VIRGO HOROSCOPE
2015

Lisa Lazuli

Lisa Lazuli is the author of the amazon bestseller

HOROSCOPE 2014: ASTROLOGY and NUMEROLOGY HOROSCOPES

ABOUT THE AUTHOR

Lisa Lazuli studied astrology with the Faculty of Astrological Studies in London.

She has practiced since 1999.

Lisa has been a regular guest on BBWM and BBC Shropshire talking about astrology and doing both horoscopes and live readings. She has also made guest appearances on Fox FM, BBC Cambridgeshire, BBC Northamptonshire, BBC Coventry and Warwickshire and US Internet Radio Shows including the Debra Clement Show.

Lisa wrote horoscopes for Asian Woman Magazine.

Now available in eBook and paperback:

TAURUS: Your Day, Your Decan, Your Sign *The most REVEALING book on The Bull yet.* Includes 2015 Predictions.

ARIES HOROSCOPE 2015

TAURUS HOROSCOPE 2015

GEMINI HOROSCOPE 2015

CANCER HOROSCOPE 2015

LEO HOROSCOPE 2015

Lisa Lazuli is also the author of

The mystery/thrillers:

A Sealed Fate

Holly Leaves

Next of Sin

As well as:

Delicious, Nutritious Recipes for the Time and Cash Strapped

Paleo Diet: Get Started, Get Motivated, Feel Great.

99 ACE Places to Promote Your Book

Pressure Cooking Reinvented.

FOREWARD

Dear Reader,

I hope my yearly horoscopes will provide you with some insightful guidance during what is a very tricky time astrologically speaking with the heavy planets i.e. Pluto and Uranus at loggerheads in cardinal signs and Neptune in Pisces calling us all to get in touch with our spiritual side.

I have a conversational style of writing, please excuse any grammatical errors, I write much as I would speak.

As the song goes, "Nobody said it was easy." I know the mass media pump-out shows us plenty about quick fix love, money, fame and success; however, life is a journey filled with challenges and obstacles designed to encourage us to find out what we are made of and who we really are.

Embrace the good and bad and enjoy what is your unique experience.

Be the hero in your own personal life movie and never hide your spotlight.

I must add that the best astrology insights are gained from a unique chart based on your time, date, year and place of birth.

If you would like your natal chart calculated for FREE, click here:

http://lisalazuli.com/2014/06/30/would-you-like-to-know-where-all-your-planets-are-free-natal-chart/

Please join me on Facebook:

https://www.facebook.com/pages/Lisa-Lazuli-Astrologer/192000594298158?ref=hl

Contents

Friendship is very important to you, and
and tested friendships that have supporte
are feeling very outgoing and are in a wo
meet new people: be they potential lover
partners. A word of warning: Virgos usu
meeting new people, and they are slow t
let that guard down too fast and be too ei
quickly – do not make that mistake. You
this year and may find you are quick to c
lend money to a friend to help out – this
a mug and get taken for a ride.

Your need for sex is strong this year but
your need for love. An indifferent or coc
will offend and hurt you. TAKE NOTE:
Virgo this year, you need to show your le
and ardent in bed; do it and say it like yc
insincerity and they can pick up anything
you will settle for no less than sincere re:
appreciation. The better the feelings of l
However terrific the sex is, it will still fa
not complete, and Virgo may call time oi
relationship if the spiritual love is not the

Virgo will call time on relationships (frie
where there is a lack of appreciation. Re
attached Virgo will fare very well if they
fully engaged and attentive – vagueness
the relationship will not go down well wi
communicate your needs to your partner
from it all – get away from distractions a
time away to each other so that you can i
intimate level.

Virgo may enjoy trying to see how much
making him/her jealous, this is one way (
tactics like this can backfire. For Virgo,

A potentially empowering time in your life, when you can use your
mental ability to focus energy and ideas to create vibrant and
constructive change in your life. You are magnetic and influential
and must use the personal power you have this year to turn the
corner and bring creative change to your relationships, health and
business relationships.

This is the year for a new outlook – it is time to ditch all those
attitudes that have not served you well. Virgos are modest and often
self-critical; your modesty is an attractive trait; however, your need
to beat up on yourself is self-defeating and often dissuades others
from cheering you on. Be your own biggest supporter and not your
biggest critic – let's face it, criticism and discouragement are not
hard to come by in life, even from those who love us, and so we
need to love and nurture ourselves and have a supportive and not a
downbeat conversation going on in our heads at all times.

Look at other attitudes and mindsets that you have, which may also
do more harm than good to both your self-confidence and your
relationships. The need to be critical and fault-finding, the need to
be working all the time, the need to go to the nth degree, the need to
worry about others and about things you cannot control. Do you
know that even though Virgos are the most health conscious of all
the signs, I have found that many Virgos smoke? Why? Because
they are often stressed out due to worry, a high degree of expectation
that they place on themselves, impossible standards or an inability to
know where to draw the line on a matter. Virgos are very vulnerable
to manipulation as they have this inbuilt desire to serve and often
feel obliged to help out or to do way beyond what they should in any
given situation. All this leads to stress. This is an excellent year to
tackle stress, but you first have to take a step back and make an
honest appraisal of the things you are doing and the people who
cause you stress. It is time to purge your life of the attitudes,
situations or people who cause anxiety in your life.

Pluto trine your Sun offers you an opportu
about your life and your life direction (mor
not like. On a spiritual level, it's a golden
lifestyle and life choices more in line with
purpose in life. Often the trine from Pluto
opportunity for change as it does not comp
via severe crisis (as with the Pluto oppositi
wait for crisis to make a change for the bet
your goals, what really matters to you. Is y
tune with who you are? Have you found y
is your life a book with the pages still blan
make your mark on the world. Be you, be
world needs. Cast off doubts, fears, fear of
do your own thing.

Making a change starts with something sm
insignificant, but if you are following your
snowball into something really important a
changing.

This a great year for making decisions as y
headspace for being rational, fair-minded a
conclusions. You are not in the mood to be
brainwashed and will hold your own and de
You are highly persuasive and diplomatic t
help you, especially in tricky or highly emc
Remember this year it's a good tactic to pre
something while secretly doing your own tl
suggesting lying or being sneaky, just play
right to stick your oar in.

Culture, art and history really interest you t
make trips to cultural capitals of the world
quench your thirst for the finer things. Virg
life, and perhaps one change you can make
art, art, languages, culture or even relations
depth than you have in the past.

often the best method, but then again, there is nothing like the
occasional cold shoulder and some space to force him/her to
appreciate you.

You are very willful this year, and your passions are closer to the
surface – you will have strong reactions to situations and to people.
You are unlikely to be undecided and passive about things; your own
feistiness and sudden zest in matters about which you were
previously indifferent can surprise you. You are very determined
and cannot be stopped once you set your mind to something. Virgos,
as a sign ruled by Mercury, are known to be adaptable and
changeable. However, this year you will be far more resolute and
less flexible in your ideas and actions. Use this year to press on with
things you would usually not have the courage to see through.
Guard against being vengeful or storing up anger against someone or
something, find ways of dealing with that anger and remove yourself
from situations that inflame you.

Health-wise, your body is sensitive now, and you must be careful of
medications and additives that may cause you a reaction. This is a
good time to go and have an allergy analysis to see if eradicating
some basic food stuffs from your diet could have a major impact on
your health and well-being.

You may be in a phase of flux in your life both mentally and
emotionally; you are changing in subtle ways, and you may not be
fully aware of what you really want next. This is an exciting yet
confusing period of your life; it is as if you are headed down a
winding road on a misty day and you cannot make out more than
100 yards ahead. That is why it is so important to make changes and
try new things this year; you have an opportunity to reinvent your
life and rewrite your future. So often in life, we think that it is all
laid out for us, like we are on a train track chugging along, then
suddenly we feel a dissatisfaction that starts as a vague feeling of
discontent, but which builds into a desire to take action even if we
are not sure what action to take. They say you don't have to know
the full plan, only the first few steps to start making a new beginning

in any aspect of life. Don't let the mist put you off setting out on something new. Part of the challenge this year is to have faith (in God, in the universe, in yourself, whichever you prefer); it is time to rediscover the part of you which is ethereal, everlasting and indestructible.

For Virgo who are spiritual or religious, this can be a significant year where your insights into life and your higher purpose are significant – events in the real world will be confusing and even surprising, but it is not with logic, but with gut feel and contemplation of the bigger picture that you can understand and get to grips with everything.

You can be vulnerable to deception and self-deception this year and so do be careful in whom you place your trust, and be aware of how your subconscious may be influencing you – always look at objective facts carefully when forming opinions as this year your usually reliable judgment can be off the mark due to emotions and subconscious influences.

While this can be a confusing year, it can be highly inspired where a crisis of identity can lead to a more refined understanding of yourself and where you want to be headed. You are slowly letting go of ego and material attachments and finding that there is a greater, spiritual sense of purpose to your life.

Virgos find it hard to let go. Your boundaries are very defined; however, this year you will be challenged to let those boundaries down, and while that can be scary, and it can open you up, it can also be very liberating. It can be a fabulous year for sexual fantasy and experiencing good sex on a whole new level.

Escapism and fantasy are very important to you. You are really feeling everything to a greater extent than usual. You are also experiencing that divine link between all human beings that unites us and so you will share in the joy, fear, loss and success of others (even those you do not know) to a far greater extent than usual. Living your life and living your life vicariously through others will have a very real meaning to you. In careers where you work with people and need to understand how it is to be in their shoes, you can have extraordinary impact on the lives of others. In medicine and veterinary work where you care for and diagnose every day, you are both accurate and perceptive. In the art world where you use words, images or even your body (i.e. dance) to convey messages, you can be highly inspired and can create work filled with emotion and relevance.

Yes, it is a time where in the midst of confusion comes the greatest clarity. Don't hold back, keep moving and keep creating change in your life. This is also a time to merge with others in terms of work and goals and experience oneness. So often in life we feel separate and different, even though we are told by the experts that we are one – this year is a lesson in commonality and how we are all really the same and that in moments of sheer joy or sadness those barriers fall away. Experiences this year will bring you close to people, even strangers perhaps, in a way you never thought possible.

You need to be more concerned about what you can see rather than what you cannot see. It is not the unknown or the secret enemies that can create obstacles for you this month, but something right under your nose, something so mundane that you could fall over it and not notice. The lesson is not to take anything in your everyday life for granted – pay attention to these things, and you will be close to avoiding problems this month.

This is in many ways a lucky month for you; unexpected pleasant surprises and developments can break up the routine and create opportunity for enjoyment, advancement and learning.

Make important arrangements and decisions or sign contracts before Jan 22 when Mercury (your ruler) turns retrograde. For any travel from Jan 22 to Fed 12 leave extra time and expect delays. If you are in the UK, finalize your tax well before the Jan 31 deadline, with Mercury retrograde you cannot afford to leave it late. Travel for business is likely, but it may be stressful and not very productive.

There is a great head and heart battle this month, with your head rather pessimistic and very earthed while your heart and intuition are actually telling you something very different about the same situations your head is so worried about. Be cautious, but do not discount what your heart is saying.

An interest in your own company and a desire to clear your head and have your own thoughts may incline you to be rather introspective this month. It is as if you need to be in touch with the inner you and get away from pleasing others, ticking boxes, clockwatching and routine chores. Bored with day-to-day life, you will escape in dystopian novels, fantasy books and movies and films favoring genres that are insightful and emotionally moving.

LOVE

You cannot abide by pettiness and controlling behavior this month – you need space, but it may not be physical as such, but mental space. Make it clear that you do not want to be nagged and dragged down to the level of the mundane all the time.

If you give each other space and avoid talking about work and problems (we all get bogged down in talking about the more irritating things in life) then things will improve as the month goes on. It is a stressful and irritating month, but you have to make your relationship a bubble where you leave those hassles on the outside – we can all switch off if we want to, it just takes more effort sometimes. Do not take the day out on each other.

The key is to make time for intimate conversations, talk more about sex, talk more about sexual fantasies, and make the time to indulge these … there is time if you make it. All work and no play, etc. …

New relationships may begin online, via Twitter or via sexting – this can be a great way to start a relationship, as sometimes it is easier to talk about sex to someone you don't know yet and who is just a name on a screen. Do always be careful and don't give out details that could come back to bite you.

In love, as in other walks of life it is the unknown which holds both excitement and opportunity for happiness this month.

CAREER

The devil is in the detail as they say – this is the key for this month. Attention to the finer points and investigating and getting to the heart of the problem is a theme. You may have to go right through a computer program or a document to find either a small glitch or tweak to get it perfect, and perfect is what is needed.

Investigation is also a key term for your workplace – extra work may come your way due to an internal investigation or office restructuring, which affects how you work and your day-to-day life. In self-employment, changes to rules and regulations may mean that you have to adjust or read through loads of paperwork to get the gist of the new requirements.

If you are looking for work, changes in your industry could also affect your qualifications, and you may have to update these and retake a test.

While these changes are annoying and not what you need, they are nowhere near as bad as they may first seem, and you will take them in your stride.

It is important to be abreast of cultural, technological and political affairs this month as they may have a direct impact on how you live and work. It may be that you have begun to take an interest in local politics or activism on something like Green issues, GM food or nuclear power. Either way, the world out there matters to you and you are realizing that you can make a difference, and you want to be heard. So if something is bugging you, get out there and meet up with others via Twitter, Facebook or meetup who have similar concerns as one voice joining with many can have a big impact.

You may be a key voice in the preserving of something important in the face of cultural and social changes – yes, evolving is inevitable, but not everything of the previous era need be cast aside.

A health issue or a health issue of someone you are close too (not necessarily a serious one, don't worry), may make you more aware of shortcomings in local health services or perhaps of a lack of information regarding a certain condition, and you may be inspired to write about, campaign about or create more awareness about this issue to help others.

Virgos are always inspired to help and to educate, and these two passions of yours are in force this month.

LOVE

The 3rd week of this month could be awesome for an explosion of passion and sexual energy – it's as if everything was pent up and suddenly you come together and whoosh, it all clicks. It is also a very social time where you feel up for meeting people, parties and perhaps movies and theatre. Although the sex can be really good, it is not very relaxing as you will tend to want and need more.

For single Virgo, the sexual attraction you feel for a new love may not last past the first few weeks and so although new relationships are quick to get going, whether they last or not is not certain and will depend on your age and expectations. If you are looking for something fun and not pinning your hopes on it, then that is great; if you are looking for more serious commitment you may be disappointed. It can be confusing as relationships that begin now have both warmth, affection and sexual excitement, so it all looks good, but are the foundations for a long term partnership really there? Be honest with yourself! Don't get carried away.

Virgos are likely to be the initiators in matters of a sexual nature and also in initiating new relationships.

CAREER

This is a very exciting month for those who work in science and technology – originality, and sudden breakthroughs are possible, and you will have a high degree of job satisfaction.

In all careers, things are moving fast and you will need to incorporate new technology and cutting edge techniques; this changeover could cause some disruption, but is well worth it and you should take the bull by the horns – the sooner you make the changes, the quicker everyone adapts.

Innovate, innovate and innovate is the key – think outside the box and have the courage to take a risk in doing something first.

Good friendships with new colleagues are a possibility. In general, you will enjoy team projects this month and can contribute with creativity and originality. However, you may lose interest if you feel others are not willing to see things through or to pull their weight. If you have any say in the team, make sure that you enlist someone who is highly pro-active and even bossy to ensure the best result.

A very good few months for those who work in alternative health, holistic fields or alternate lifestyles.

There is a big focus on interpersonal communication, both intimate and business. The way you see yourself is affected both positively and indeed, negatively, but those you are close to or those you associate with business-wise. They say you are judged by the company you keep and somehow this month actions of those you are associated with will have more of an impact on you than your own actions. This is why you need to choose your business associates with care and be careful about who you hang out with socially. It is not always possible to disconnect ourselves with everyone whose behavior may reflect on us, but do be aware and ready to limit damage when necessary.

Relationships can be a great area of learning and self-evolvement this month – we often dislike people who have traits that we do not like in ourselves, so it is worth examining those who you take a dislike to and asking yourself what they can teach you about yourself and how you can change for the better.

We also attract people who are similar to us and are having similar thoughts to us – we are a reverse magnet where like does indeed attract like. You may well attract a person into your life that mirrors your own emotional life – this person can be a very helpful sounding board for you to confide in, although they may not necessarily become a friend.

The solar eclipse this month will strengthen relationships that are solid and rewarding while it may tip relationships that are unbalanced and unsatisfying over the edge. This applies to all relationships.

Harmony and balance are very important to your emotional growth, and you will strive for this in all your intimate contacts – but remember, you cannot be all things to all people.

LOVE

Closeness and relationship success is linked to self-esteem more than usual this month. Virgo and Scorpio are signs that are the happiest single and yet, single Virgos will feel inadequate this month and will yearn for a close relationship.

Married Virgos who feel their relationships are not going as well as they should, may also suffer from feelings of inadequacy and self-criticism. There are a couple of things to remember: Virgos have very high standards which are not always possible to meet, and Virgos are highly discriminating which can hinder relationship formation, and there is nothing wrong with that. However, you cannot compare yourself to people who get into relationships easily as they are less discriminating. In relationships, Virgo may overlook the good and spend too much time concentrating on the negative. Number two: relationships are dynamic, they grow and one must expect ups and downs and not a flat line. Relationships are a mirror on which to reflect on ourselves for the purpose of growth, not to be self-critical.

Your relationships are the means by which you increase your human understanding and get to grips with deep emotional complexes; they are also a way in which you can transcend your own limitations – which is often why Virgos attract the exact opposite to them (in terms of relationships) so you can live vicariously through your significant other and their experiences.

Self-worth may be experienced through helping a partner who is unwell or struggling with an emotional or physical issue. Single Virgo may be attracted to someone vulnerable or in need of help.

CAREER

Business partnership and alliances (other than the caveat in the first paragraph) can be a hugely valuable way of opening up new doors for your business or within your career. In this case teaming up with someone with very different competencies, can help you expand quickly or gain confidence.

There can be a sudden turnabout in legal cases you are involved in for the better.

A good month for implementing new systems to get more organized or to track your finances more effectively. Try and streamline your payments and use this month to look over your costs to see where savings can be made. You are clever with numbers this month and so do the sums and see where you can arrange things to get more for your buck. Check those bank statements and use comparison sites to get better deals for insurance, etc.

A very good month for those who write or teach about issues to do with health, hygiene or scientific subjects.

Be purposeful and make sure everything you do has a direct payback or function – do not waste time and money this month on things that have an unproven value to you or your business.

LIFE

This is a period where your enthusiasm and boldness will allow you to take up challenges that you may usually shy away from. You are restless and unlikely to be passive and let life control you; you want to shape things this month and will not take a back seat and let others or circumstances dictate events.

You may book a spontaneous break away – perhaps a camping, walking or sporting trip with friends or a partner. You are very active and want to make every second count. This is not a month for lazing about; you are motivated and can use your positive energy to bring enjoyment and fun into your life.

Do not waste your increased mental and physical energy this month – this is an ideal time to begin new studies, brush up on skills, start a course and/or learn a new sport. Use April to improve your skills and fitness, then the month is more about fun with purpose than just fun.

Restless and assertive, you will rebel against restrictions and limits which you feel are unreasonable and restrictive.

Try not to get fired up and get into arguments over religious or philosophical issues as these are likely to become contentious and unpleasant with no real purpose.

LOVE

Opportunities for both success and social networking can come via your partner this month – perhaps an opportunity to change job or get new clients can come via a social event arranged for your partner's work.

You are very romantic this month and also compassionate and flexible – you are willing to adjust to the needs of your partner and this bodes well for love. You are more relaxed in general during April, which means that sex will flow naturally, and nothing will need to be forced.

There is a new sense of devotion within your relationship; the longer you have been together, the more you will appreciate each other this month as there is a sense of shared experience and warmth of emotion stemming from what you have been through and shared over the years.

This is a very positive month for couples who work together, either in business or some form of venture. Events will push you together as you are required to focus on some shared goal of mutual importance.

In-laws may be a problem this month – be firm with them, and do not let them interfere.

CAREER

This can be a very opportune month to make a good impression on your boss or those of influence at your company – accept all positions of organizational and managerial responsibility, do not turn up a chance to do a different role due to modesty. Unlike what the CEO of Microsoft recently said, this IS a good time to ask for a raise or to negotiate a better pay deal or superior benefits – don't leave it up to karma as good karma also favors those who are not passive. Be bold and put in for a transfer or promotion or get a conversation going with HR about your career development.

A very good month for those in modeling and careers where beauty and grace are important, i.e. dance, ballet, acting.

Diplomacy and bridge-building are very important career-wise and so be the one to put out an olive branch to colleagues or perhaps business rivals with whom you have clashed in the past.

In your job or business, structure your month so that you get cracking on new deals, new initiatives and promotional activity at the start of the month, leave admin work, organizational work and financial work until the last third of the month. The first third of April is best for taking chances and being proactive, while the last third is better for playing it safe and getting back to basics, i.e. ensuring the most important facets of the business are running smoothly.

LIFE

There is a lot of nervous tension this month. You are irritable and find delays very frustrating. It can be hard to avoid being rubbed up the wrong way by people and especially the way they choose to communicate. Choose your words carefully and delay decisions if you can, as you may make an inappropriate choice in haste. Be careful of what you commit to by email or social media as once things are out there, it can be hard to get them back.

It is a busy time for admin, i.e. forms to fill in, correspondence to take care of, contracts to draw up and buying and selling, but it will not necessarily go smoothly as Mercury turns retrograde on the 19th, so best to get things finalized before then.

Others may try to stir up controversy with you, do not rise to provocation – the calmer you remain, the better for you and your own purposes.

It is very important to remain flexible in your thinking and also within your routine as this month is highly unpredictable, and facts or circumstances will change quickly and with little notice.

LOVE

Although, as an earth sign, Virgos find physicality in a relationship very important, Virgos also crave intellectual stimulation and talking and exchanging ideas is vital to the life of the relationship. This is the time where the friendship part of your marriage/relationship is very important. You need to rediscover that bond of mutual interest and reignite conversation and chat within the marriage. How much time do you spend talking, how much time do you spend doing things together? This month is great to get involved socially together, either with friends or doing something you both find enjoyable and fulfilling.

Doing activities together is a great way to renew relationships and get them back on track – when you drift apart that communication breaks down further and further, but when you get involved in things together, the intellectual side of the relationship will get going again, and this is fundamental to love and the health of your relationships.

Single Virgo will seek a new partner who is an intellectual and social equal – which is why meeting new potential lovers via your friends or interest groups is the best way to find a good match right now.

CAREER

Money is not a huge issue to Virgo; yes of course, without it what can we do? but in terms of career, Virgos like to feel as if they are making a difference and doing something constructive for either humanity or the environment. This motivation is very strong in Virgo this month and is why Virgo can excel in careers like nursing, medicine, research, teaching or healing. You have an extra special ability to diagnose or find appropriate solutions to complex and baffling problems. Your ability to see to the heart of the matter and apply such commitment to what you do is inspiring, even in difficult situations.

An excellent month for Virgos, who work with their hands for either healing i.e. physio or chiropracting or perhaps something like jewelry making or crafting.

Another feature of this month is putting in the hours, not for any direct benefit, but because you have the belief in what you are doing. Belief is a strong driver for your actions this month, both at home and work. You may also stick up for the underdog or give a voice to someone who has none.

LIFE

This is a month when you are highly subjective in your thinking, and so it is not a good time to make decisions where you have to be very methodical and objective. If you do have to focus on facts, make sure that you do just that as the temptation right now is to ignore concrete evidence and go with your emotional reaction, which may not really be reliable. You are very vulnerable to outside influences right now and so what you are feeling may be colored by those you are with or perhaps media influences – step away from these influences and perhaps you will see things differently.

The temptation is to go with the flow this month – not to think for yourself, but to piggyback on the thoughts and ideas of others – this is not the best way for you and may lead you off in the wrong direction. There is also an inclination to go off on tangents that may lead you into cul- de-sacs. Now sometimes a tangent can be quite exciting, but if you have limited time, I would suggest looking at everything critically before you pursue it, as not everything is what it seems this month, and what may look like terrific opportunities may well be a waste of time.

Boost your immune and nervous system this month with vitamin B complex and vitamin D. Get plenty of sunshine and take moderate exercise – this is not a good month for strenuous activity or physical training.

LOVE

Highly imaginative and willing to let go, this is a great month just to drop your guard and fall in love. Single Virgo will have a very strong desire to socialize and form new romantic connections – you may find lovers are like buses, all coming at once, and you may want to keep your options open.

This month you are putting a lot of energy into creative projects and hobbies, and it is via these that you can meet new love interests. More open-minded and indeed seeking diversity, you may attract someone totally different, who you would never have thought you could get on with.

You are very generous and open-hearted right now – willing to forgive and forget and happy to move on from small or even medium disagreements for the sake of harmony. Things are going well in all relationships. You are very positive now in your attitude, and this makes it easy for you to focus on the good and put the negative into perspective. It is not that you want to iron things out right now; you simply want to move on and to see the bigger picture.

This is a happy and contented month where you look at issues within your relationship with wisdom and acceptance; somehow, you are seeing things philosophically, and it is giving you a new perspective. Not all issues can be sorted out logically or via communication, some must simply be consigned to the past and grown out of.

You are keen to pamper and spoil yourself at this time – but overdoing the spending or eating could be a sign that you are looking for satisfaction in the wrong places.

CAREER

Yes, you are a bit lazy this month – we'll blame the summer should we? Mentally, you are a little checked out right now, almost as if the holidays have begun. It will be hard to focus on mundane and routine tasks, and you will really need to muster all your self-discipline to enable you to deal with these. On the other hand, if you are dealing with issues to do with promotion, customer relations, meeting new clients, staff training, motivational workshops or work-related travel, you should feel far more inspired and can be very productive.

Be careful about how you spend money – be it business or personal investment opportunities. This is a good time to invest in your business or stocks; however, you are a little over optimistic right now and so be sure to rein that in when you make your decisions.

You may be planning an exotic vacation at this time or even a business trip that is more about pleasure than business – just make sure that you do not over-extend your credit card.

On a serious note, if you do take out a loan with a financial plan, do be sure that your predictions and forecasts are accurate and not overly optimistic – make sure you take everything into account and plan for contingencies.

LIFE

Diplomacy and the intellectualizing of problems are very important this month. It's not what you say but how you say it that counts, and you must be both tactful and mindful of other values and issues when you broach subjects.

Seeking compromise and middle ground is as beneficial to you as to others, and so it is the best way forward this month. You can be very indecisive this month, and it is best to take time for some detailed pro and con weighting before you commit to a choice – you may need to explain yourself later, and so the more you can convey how you weighed the options and what you took into account, the better for you.

You are highly persuasive in July and your ability to see the other side and play devil's advocate can really help you to nail a deal or convince someone of something.

LOVE

The focus on communication within your relationships returns this month. Being on the same wavelength as your partner is vital to the health of your relationship, and you are looking to revitalize this element. You need more intellectual stimulation; you want the sole attention of your partner, not attention divided between you, the iPad, the iPhone, etc.

If the communication is not of the quality you expect, look to yourself for answers – have you been too critical? Have you been trying to score points rather than actually listening to what your partner has to say? Has your partner given up trying to talk to you as you over-analyze or rationalize away problems. Often Virgos are very analytical when perhaps all your lover wants to hear is "poor thing" or "that's horrible." Sometimes when someone pours their heart out they want sympathy and a hug, not analysis or being told why their problem is not really a problem. Learn to give people what they want when they share, rather than what you think they need. Often people just want to talk to get it out, and they don't find a barrage of advice that helpful.

Love and understanding should be the focus of communication this month rather than detailed analysis.

CAREER

Focus on work that delivers concrete and verifiable results. Improve communication between colleagues and also in terms of vertical communication – chase things up, and if you do not hear from someone, get back to them and hurry them on.

You may decide to take a sabbatical, i.e. take time off work to pursue more training or arrange with your employers to sponsor you to study on to improve your prospects.

Many Virgos will be on vacation this month or experiencing a slowdown at work. If you are still at work, use this time to promote yourself and business via social networks – ensure all your profiles are up-to-date and improve SEO for your enterprise. This is an excellent time to highlight your businesses achievements in the local press; you may also want to hook up with other local business to pool funds for promo and advertising.

It is very important that you are in tune with social trends and mores and so immerse yourself in magazines and the popular press so that you know what is going on – you cannot get away with being out of touch no matter what you do.

You can achieve more via creating synergies with similar business this month.

A very productive and enjoyable time at work for accountants, broadcasters, PAs, promoters and those who work in consumer products.

LIFE

This marks the beginning of a golden year of opportunity, marked by Jupiter's entry into the sign of Virgo. This is a time where you will be optimistic, gung-ho and positive about life. You are more secure with your self-image and happier within yourself. You are projecting in an open, wholehearted way and will attract new people and new experiences into your life, which will benefit your life goals.

You will experience a renewed sense of purpose in life, and this will help you make decisions that will help broaden your scope of experience. There will be the chance for travel and also further learning.

Your health will improve, and if you have had poor health or injuries, you will now convalesce quickly. Mentally, your attitude is much more positive, and you will have the inner strength to move on from negative situations and habits which have hampered your life in the past.

You are likely to meet many new people in the next few months, and these people will enrich your life and also bring a new element of understanding to you.

Everything in moderation is the key as Jupiter benefits us by making us expansive in our thinking and attitudes, but on the negative side, we can overdo things, and you know that too much of a good thing is also bad.

LOVE

Jupiter is benefitting your love life.

Single Virgos are likely to attract benevolent, outgoing and progressive types. This is a time when someone you meet could really bring you out of yourself and awaken you to new facets of yourself.

In established relationships, you are eager for change – change for the better. You want to renew the relationships and re-experience the fire, you will be the driving force behind encouraging you to do new things as a couple and reignite your social life.

The only downside to relationships this month is managing expectations – the earth can't move every time, no matter who you are.

CAREER

In keeping with the themes of this month, it is a good time to look at where you can take your career or business further, and if you are unemployed, certainly look to jazz up your CV and start looking for jobs again. Take a look back at any plans you have shelved and give them a second thought. Things that did not work in the past due to circumstances, you may now be better placed to attempt again.

In life, you have to catch the wave; you may have been wading in still water but now the waves are rolling in, and you need to be ready to catch one.

It is best to be coy about your plans and keep them to yourself, you do not want to be put off track by negativity from Debbie Downers or those who are jealous and want to hold you back.

LIFE

Independence and freedom of both thought and movement and your right to express yourself is vehemently defended this month.

The tempo of life's events is fast and furious right now, you will not be able to sit back and relax as things will be happening, the phone will be ringing, and life can take some surprising turns. It is an exciting time of much communication and interaction with others. You will have to be adaptable and able to respond to changing situations quickly. This is a time of surprise, and you can be jolted out of your comfort zone, but this is a good thing as often the comfort zone is the biggest block to potential.

This month is a chance to take a new and stimulating view of life and to renew your thinking on many issues. Experimentation with new activities, ideas, people and places is likely – you are spontaneous and may surprise others with your actions at times.

Events can be hard to keep track of with so much going on, so do be sure to keep a diary so that you do not overlook important dates and deadlines. It is also a month of little sleep and minimal time to relax as even if you are off from work, you are bound to be travelling, organizing or busy with a hectic home life. Make sure you do fit in some time when the phone goes off along with the internet connection, so you have a clear head space to center yourself. The biggest threat this month is that you lose your way due to a commotion in your life; you may become so involved in so many things that it all becomes a chaotic and unproductive cacophony. Keep focus by sticking to an overall plan, and even if it is impossible to stick to that plan, at least do not lose sight of it.

LOVE

Stability and consistency are what is important to you in love relationships this month – the more you feel that your partner is a rock or support, the more your relationships will run smoothly. If you feel your partner is flakey or fickle that can be a real source of aggravation. You have no time for mixed messages and games – you want your love life to be straightforward and to know where you are.

You do have a lot on your plate, and you are not patient with your partner right now – you expect him/her to be an adult and to step up to the plate. You will be very frustrated if your partner does not share and take responsibility for things as they indeed should. If you are working as a team and supporting each other, then this is a good time for your relationship, even if it is not especially romantic. However, if you feel like you are carrying the relationship and also all the burdens, you will become distant and cool with your loved one. This is a tipping point for relationships which have become unbalanced and where there are double standards.

Single Virgo are looking for some answers in new relationships – you want to know if it is going anywhere and whether the relationship has potential. This is the point where you decide whether it goes further or if you call it a day, either way you want to move forward not stay where you are.

CAREER

This month it is important to make networking work for you – yes, it's great setting up contacts and meeting potential clients, but now you must cement those relationships and make them profitable.

In all aspects of your career-making linkages, drawing disparate elements together and making the parts of what you do contribute to the end product is important. You must actualize ideas and begin to make them concrete.

There is quite a degree of pressure to produce results this month – you may have to write up reports, finish stories, do your accounts, etc. You may have to report in detail about why profits were down or costs were up, and you will have to investigate these and look for answers. You see it is all about looking at the parts in detail and then seeing how they relate to the final analysis.

You may be overwhelmed by errands and communications, and you need to weed out what is important and what is not – lucky Virgos are very good at that!

What you want to avoid this month is defining yourself in terms of others or in relation to others. Do not be caught in the Facebook trap of thinking everyone else is doing great and having a fab life then feeling rather inadequate about yourself and your achievements. We live in an age of hyperbole; Facebook is just like a shop window where only the best is on display and the broken, soiled wares are hidden in the storeroom. Do not be taken in by it – it is comparing yourself to a much-exaggerated model, which is fake in reality.

You are aiming for comfort and peace this month, and yet you seem to be attracting complicated circumstances into your life that are making you ill at ease. You need a certain detachment, and you need to develop some distance from the other's problems, even if you care about that person, you cannot take on their issues to the exclusion of your own concerns.

As much as helping others empowers you and satisfies you, you cannot develop your self-worth via others alone. Define your goals in terms of your own values and not those of others. Learn to be more patient with yourself and more sympathetic towards yourself.

What I have said above applies for the next few months, starting now.

LOVE

Making decisions that accommodate both of your values and priorities can be a challenge this month, especially when it comes to decisions to do with your children – there will have to be debate and some compromises. However, it need not be all or nothing – the best solutions are mindful of both sets of priorities and opinions.

Money is key – there may be arguments about the joint bank account and how to spend money. Be honest and do not try and conceal the money you spent on that dress or that part for your motorbike.

Money can also be used as a tool to manipulate or a bargaining tool – do not fall into that trap. It's not about how much you both bring in as not everything you bring to the table has a monetary value and many vital elements in a relationship cost time and effort, not money.

If you can get beyond material matters and mundane considerations then you are in for a treat as this can be a great month for good sex and sexual healing. When it clicks in the bedroom, the other problems fall away.

CAREER

Getting your taxes and VAT in order this month should be a priority, but so should investigating how restructuring your spending could help you save tax. On an individual basis, seek some tax advice from a specialist or from the tax department to see if you are eligible for any savings or if you could improve your tax outlook via a change in pension plan, etc. Remember tax laws change nearly every year, and you never know when a change can benefit you or your business. Use reputable forums to get advice online and then take action.

If you work with other people's money, i.e. in accounting, investments, trust funds, as a purser, in realty etc. you will have added responsibility and must be accountable for all aspects so be careful if you delegate.

You can use your sexual magnetism and charm to your advantage in business this month – now it is up to you how you would use this, but be aware that you are exuding an animal magnetism right now, and so why not turn it to your advantage? Women and men can benefit. It's a jungle out there, use any leverage you have when you have it.

LIFE

Sometimes we work hard and do not see much reward, but this month your hard work will pay off and with patience you can build on previous efforts and feel a sense of achievement and accomplishment. You may not feel as if you are setting the world alight, but your efforts are enduring and what you work towards now has a lasting quality to it – i.e. it may be something important which you can put on your CV, a qualification or a life landmark for you personally.

This month is perfect for both spiritual and intellectual growth as you can see the necessity for some of the more challenging or inhibiting aspects of your life; you are able to see meaning within the troubles you face. Sometimes we rebel or lash out to feel that we are empowered, but this month you are aware of how the structures in your life (however annoying they may be) play a role in making you secure and giving you a solid base. Virgos, ruled by Mercury are by nature restless; however, as an earth sign you crave stability and a certain routine – reconciling these disparate elements of your personality can take time and maturity, and you may have phases where you swing from one to the other. This month it is easier for you to combine and experience the benefits of both.

The impact of the planets right now is to create subtle effects that may not actually be appreciated in terms of their worth until months later.

LOVE

A loving, generous and spontaneous attitude will help your love life to flow both in new and older relationships. This month, you are feeling young again, and this is what is helping you to find new and exciting ways to experience love and affection. The teenager in you is alive again, and you are appreciating life more as you feel you can let your hair down and enjoy life without all the baggage that one usually feels weighed down with.

Sensually you are more attuned to your environment, and everything seems to look brighter, music sounds better and things taste better than usual – this is wonderful as sexually you are so much more receptive to touch, feel and movement. Take your time over sex this month, read some erotic books and try using massage oils and giving each other massages and foot massages, etc. I do not want to be too explicit, but stimulate all the senses during sex and take your time to immerse yourselves in each other.

This is an excellent month for Virgo to meet new partners; you are social, charming and fun-loving – free of the inhibitions you usually have, you are quick to make new friends and romantic opportunities will come your way as you are very open right now. New relationships that arise should be very active, i.e. you will be going out a lot, socializing with each other's friends, attending parties and going to theatre/movies and events.

CAREER

This is a very favorable time for planning as you have the ability to keep a handle on the broad range goals as well as the details. You can work hard on things that may seem too insignificant or boring to your colleagues for them to bother about – but your attention to these things can bring you recognition from your employer.

This month may not be about individuality and proving yourself; you may get more control or influence in the longer term by working diligently in the background. Your efforts will be noticed even if you are not making a song and dance about it – working on in your modest way will pay dividends.

Creatively, you are very expressive right now and feel freer to go beyond your normal scope in terms of what you produce. You can show leadership on artistic projects right now.

This is a very favorable time for Virgos who are involved in hospitality and the entertainment field – you will have many new customers and be very successful with all your events. This is also an opportune time for Virgos who are looking to launch something, i.e. a fashion range, book production, home wares, art, etc.

LIFE

You are mischievous, and your sense of humor is also in top gear. Virgos are terrific raconteurs and during the holiday especially, when you see people you have not seen for a while; what a great time to use this talent to regale them with the events of your life this year.

With a little extra time to spare, you are very much in the mood for games be it chess, crosswords, Sudoku or other mentally stimulating games. Virgos enjoy the stimulation of puzzles and word games – you may even find yourself hooked on some phone apps that allow you to learn new games.

You may enjoy making cards and gifts this holiday season to give them that personal touch. This is a very good month for work involving crafts, i.e. artwork, card making, woodwork, pottery, textiles, dressmaking, etc. Perhaps you will get roped into making props or costumes for the children's nativity play – this can be great fun and should not be shied away from as it can be very therapeutic.

You'll enjoy physical challenges this month and may take part in fun runs or energetic exercise in preparation for any pounds you'll be putting on once the holiday eating begins.

You can be quite impulsive about spending this December so keep the receipts and make sure of the return policy so at least if you do have a change of mind you can return.

This is a very positive month to start thinking about next year, especially in relation to money, i.e. new ways to make money, save money, invest money or ideas for second income streams. In fact, be on the lookout for business opportunities/ideas that may present themselves this Christmas.

LOVE

Virgos are again in the mood for romance, and it is quite possible that you may be feeling broody and want to start or extend your family – you will talk much about children this December.

This month you are very eloquent when it comes to expressing romantic feelings, and so perhaps your gift to your partner could be a series of poems or love letters. Whatever your feelings for your partner, it is important to express them verbally, as the song goes:

"Tell her about it, let her know just how you feel, give her every reason to accept that you're for real."

We all get insecure in relationships, and this is your chance to tell the one you love how special they are and how their love and support means everything to you. Mention specific things that he/she does that you especially like or enjoy, both physical and mental traits. Never think that, "I don't have to say that 'cause he/she knows how I feel!" People invariably don't know how you feel, and they want to hear it anyway – a "Thank you for being you!" goes an awful long way in any relationship.

Single Virgos are both charming and very witty this month, making it easy for them to attract new partners. Again, there may be more than one on the go. You are very curious this month and eager to broaden your catchment criteria in terms of men/women – you may well be attracted to someone other than your type. The interest you take in finding out all about your new love is key to getting things off to a great start; people love it when you want to hear about them and their life, too many people talk too much about themselves.

CAREER

Many Virgos who are still studying may begin to think about careers involving children this December. This may influence subjects you choose in future or work placements you look for in the summer. Often one has to start applying for your summer/July jobs in January so it is worth thinking ahead about what you would like to do and researching employers who are taking staff on.

Client and customer communication is vital this December: do not neglect to wish clients for the holidays and lay on special discounts, bargains and offers for your customers. Christmas and the holidays provide an excellent opportunity to cement good relationships as well as giving you the chance to touch base with all your clients/customers both new and old.

Whatever work you are in, take time to wish those in your Facebook groups or LinkedIn network well for the New Year – this is your chance to say HI, REMEMBER ME. In networking, you never know who you can ask a question or create an opportunity with in the New Year. No one likes being contacted only when you need them, but if you have always wished them well over the holidays, it creates a feeling that you touch base with them often and remember them fondly.

Well-wishing and Christmas greetings play a vital role in business and is also a chance to cement good relations with colleagues – you spend eight hours a day at work, you may as well get on with people there and foster a good spirit.

Look after everyone that makes your business tick this Christmas.

Have a FABULOUS 2016 and may the force of the planets be with you!

CPSIA information can be obtained at www.ICGtesting.com
Printed in the USA
LVOW04s1646120115

422499LV00001B/382/P